INTRODUC'

Many people believe that black and Asi‹
part in life in Britain before the Second W
and Asian people have been coming to liv   … this
country for centuries. Despite being the v   _ ‹ı discrimination,
persecution and enslavement they have, throughout this time, made
an important contribution to our society.

A proclamation by Queen Elizabeth I, in 1601 which refers
disparagingly to "the great numbers of negars and Blackamores which
… are crept into this realm" confirms the fact that, even in the
sixteenth century, black people were present in England. In the
seventeenth and eighteenth centuries, West Indian planters returning
to this country brought black slaves with them to wait on them and
their families. Government officials, army officers and wealthy
merchants brought in Asians from India. Black Africans arrived,
principally as slaves but also, in some cases, as free men engaged to
man British ships.

Even in the early seventeenth century, in addition to serving as
household servants and in other menial capacities, a minority of the
black population made a modest contribution to cultural life. Black
musicians played in musical entertainments and military bands and
others performed in pageants, like that of the Lord Mayor of London
and similar dramatic events. In 1773 poems on various subjects,
religious and moral, by Phyllis Wheatley, a young slave woman from
Boston, New England, visiting London with her mistress's son, received
favourable reviews in numerous learned journals. The letters of
Ignatius Sancho, a former slave, who became a friend of Samuel
Johnson, Laurence Sterne and others well known in literary and artistic
circles, were published in 1782, two years after his death. He was
known for his poems, musical compositions and love of the theatre.

Others became known for their public opposition to slavery. Ottobah
Cuguano, who came from a part of West Africa now within Ghana,
published 'Thoughts and Sentiments on the Evil and wicked Traffic
of the Slavery and Commerce of the Human Species' in 1787. He
called for the outlawing of the slave trade and the emancipation of
the slaves. Olaudah Equiano, from what is today Nigeria, also
campaigned against slavery and wrote 'The Interesting Narrative of

the Life of Olaudah Equiano or Gustavus Vassa, the African,' published in 1789. He became a member of Thomas Hardy's London Corresponding Society, the first real working class political reform organisation, established in 1792.

William Davidson, a radical activist from Kingston, Jamaica, was hanged for his part in the 1819 Cato Street Conspiracy. Another black advocate of radical reform, Robert Wedderburn, suffered imprisonment for views he expressed a few years later. William Cuffay, whose father came from St. Kitts, became one of the leaders of the Chartist Movement, which campaigned for the right of all men to vote.

Bill Miller, the subject of this study, was in this tradition. The son of a seaman and grandson of a slave, he was a leading member of Plymouth Council for over forty years. Even before the First World War, John Archer, a black Liverpuddlian, had become Mayor of Battersea in 1913/14, illustrating the fact that members of the black community could overcome the obstacles that faced them in public life. Since then, of course, many more have made the breakthrough.

Bill Miller's story is part of this struggle for the emancipation of people who have been discriminated against and downtrodden for centuries. It is also, however, part of the struggle of working people, regardless of origin, to improve their conditions of life. As this pamphlet reveals, both Bill and his son, Claude, have made an immense contribution to this cause in Plymouth.

This study is an extended version of an address given by Jonathan Wood in Plymouth in July 2001, at an event sponsored by Labour Heritage, with the support of the Black and Asian Studies Association (BASA), to commemorate Bill Miller's life. It aimed to fulfil the objectives for which Labour Heritage was created: to pursue and perpetuate the history of the Labour Movement and its activists. It is evident from the text that Jonathan Wood has fully achieved these objectives.

Bill Miller's life of dedicated endeavour has been recorded in these pages for the benefit and enlightenment of all who read them now and, hopefully, in future years.

It is an enthralling story.

Stan Newens

Chair - Labour Heritage

LABOUR HERITAGE

✦ encourages an interest among Labour Party members and others in the history of the Labour Party and labour movement.

✦ promotes the preservation of the records of the labour movement at national and local level and encourages their study.

✦ ensures that the history of ordinary people within the Labour Party and trade union movement is not forgotten and that working men and women have a chance to study and record their own history.

✦ produces a Bulletin and organises themed talks at its Annual General Meetings and other events.

You can help by joining Labour Heritage
Membership is open to Labour Party members and others interested in Party history. We particularly welcome affiliations from constituency and branch Labour Parties, and trade unions. Labour Heritage is able to provide speakers on many aspects of Labour history for local meetings. In addition we can advise on the preservation of Party and trade union records.

Subscription rates

£10.00- waged	£12.00 - joint waged
£4.00 - unwaged	£6.00 - joint unwaged
£20.00- Labour Parties and Trade Unions	£25.00 - organisations

Further details on: www.labourheritage.com
To contact Labour Heritage email: GriggShampan1@ukonline.co.uk

BILL MILLER
Black Labour Party Activist in Plymouth

Introduction

In 1952, a writer, Laurence Thompson, had a lengthy discussion with Councillor William Alexander Miller, Chairman of Plymouth City Council's Housing Committee and the leading figure in the Council's ambitious housing programme. For Bill Miller the new housing estates which had been built during his chairmanship of the Committee were not merely meeting the desperate need for houses in his heavily-bombed city but were providing the basis for social change. When he was asked if the tenants of the new estates would be able to pay the rents, Bill Miller responded ' It means they must go without some things - they can't go greyhound racing or do the pools, or smoke twenty cigarettes a day or buy monster comics … We're building a new race of people who won't want to do those things. You must see it. They won't want amusements made for them. They'll make their own amusements in the community centres, in the schools with their children… They can pay, they will pay, if you give them something worth paying for.'[1]

As these words indicate, Bill Miller was a visionary and a visionary who was able to turn his visions into reality. While he was Chair of the Housing Committee, Plymouth's housebuilding programme was, in proportion to the city's size, one of the largest in England. Bill was also Plymouth's first black councillor, in a city with a tiny ethnic minority population. His career in the Labour Party and the trade union movement was one of outstanding public service and personal sacrifice and he deserves to be better remembered.[2]

Bill Miller's origins and early life

Bill's ancestors were Africans who lived in Sierra Leone. His grandfather was a slave who was granted his freedom at a church mission in Sierra Leone. Bill Miller's father left home, found employment on a British ship and came to England where he married an Englishwoman. He eventually settled in Stonehouse which in the late 19th century was one of three adjacent and closely linked towns - Plymouth, Stonehouse and Devonport.

Bill Miller was born in East Street, Stonehouse on 15th July 1890. After his education in local schools, he worked first in the building industry and then in the electrical department of Devonport Dockyard, the largest and most important employer in the Three Towns.[3-6]

In 1914 there was a major change in the structure of local government in the area. The three towns of Plymouth, Stonehouse and Devonport had, in physical terms, become a single conurbation but remained separate politically with their own councils. In 1914, after the people of the three communities had voted for amalgamation in a referendum, the three towns merged to form the Corporation of Plymouth. Plymouth became a city in 1928.[7, 8]

In August 1914, Britain entered the First World War. During the war Bill Miller served in the Royal Flying Corps and rose to the rank of warrant officer.[3]

Plymouth Labour Movement following the First World War
In the parliamentary reorganisation of 1918, Plymouth was divided into three parliamentary constituencies - Devonport, Drake and Sutton.[9]

After the war, Bill Miller returned to Devonport Dockyard where he worked as an electrician in the Dockyard's electrical department. He became a prominent activist in his union, the Electrical Trades Union (ETU), and eventually became President of the Devon and Cornwall area of the ETU.

Bill Miller was also extremely active in the Plymouth Labour Party. He became Secretary of the Drake Divisional Labour Party and the party's election agent. In the 1920s several of the leading trade unionists in Devonport Dockyard played major roles in the Plymouth Labour Party. These men were James John Moses, usually referred to as Jimmy Moses, a leading figure in the Shipwrights' and Ship Constructors' Association in the Dockyard, H. M. (Bert) Medland, full-time secretary and leader of the Engineers' union in the Dockyard, and Henry George (Harry) Mason who had been a friend of Bill since their schooldays. Bill worked closely with these men in the Labour Party's campaigns in the city.[5, 10]

In the years following the First World War, the Labour Party's political support and influence grew dramatically and the first Labour government was elected in 1924. The rise of the Labour Party nationally was paralleled by Labour's advance in Plymouth. During the 1920s, increasing numbers of Labour Councillors were elected in Plymouth and in 1926 Jimmy Moses became the city's first Labour Mayor.

Bill Miller was prominent in Plymouth Labour in these years. In the General Elections of 1923 and 1924, Jimmy Moses stood as the Labour candidate in the Drake constituency and Bill was his election agent. He was able and hard-working with impressive organisational skills. He was elected to Plymouth City Council in 1925 and became an alderman in 1927. [3, 6, 10]

Labour wins Plymouth Drake constituency
Jimmy Moses had been impressed by Bill's work in the General Elections of 1923 and 1924. He appointed him as his election agent when he contested the Drake Division in the General Election of 1929. Jimmy Moses was victorious in the General Election, winning 16,884 votes compared with the 14,572 votes for his Conservative opponent, and became Plymouth's first Labour M.P. [11]

The Drake Election Petition
However, Jimmy Moses' election victory was challenged in the courts. Political opponents presented a parliamentary election petition stating that the election in Plymouth Drake should be declared null and void because Moses' victory had been achieved by the use of bribery and corrupt practices. Petitions challenging the validity of an election were rare and this was the first time in the Labour Party's history that an election petition of this kind had been brought against one of its members.

The most serious allegations concerned the activities of Albert Ballard, a wealthy philanthropist who had come to Plymouth some years previously and who financed and organised social, sporting and educational activities for boys in which thousands of Plymothian lads participated. Ballard had been an enthusiastic and vocal supporter of Jimmy Moses and had offered rewards to the boys who attended his clubs with the intention that this would encourage them to influence their parents to vote for Mr Moses. Another of the allegations directly implicated Bill. It was claimed that, in his role as Moses' election agent, he had allowed a private hire car to be used in the Drake election campaign which was a breach of electoral law.

Bill prepared for this difficult legal case with great thoroughness. Plymouth Labour Party was very fortunate that Sir Stafford Cripps, a distinguished lawyer and a Labour Party member, offered to defend Jimmy Moses for free. The case of the election petition against Moses was held in a specially constituted court in the Plymouth Guildhall in October 1929. Bill was one of the witnesses called to give evidence. Cripps' defence of Moses was a powerful one and the judges dismissed the election petition. This was a great relief for Bill for whom the case had been a gruelling and stressful experience. [9, 12, 13]

Political Activities in the 1930s

Jimmy Moses was Drake's M.P. for a relatively short period of time. In the General Election of 1931, when the Labour Party nationally suffered the most disastrous electoral defeat in its history, he lost his seat, beaten by a margin of over 12,000 votes.

Despite the adverse political climate of the decade, Bill Miller established an impressive reputation in local politics. He was a member of a number of Council committees: Allotments and Cemeteries, Electricity and Street Lighting, Tramways and Stores. His work on these committees was imaginative and innovative. He introduced the first electricity showrooms, the first free electrical wiring service and the first cremations. He took part in the opening of Tinside Pool, a well-known open-air swimming pool on Plymouth Hoe, on 2 October 1935. The pool was once known as 'Miller's Lido'.

Bill was exceptionally conscientious in his work for local people. His son, Claude, a City Councillor who was recently Lord Mayor, remembers queues of people outside their house in East Street, Stonehouse, waiting to see his father. Bill became known as 'the Poor Man's Lawyer'. He devoted great time and energy to his council activities and his family had to cope on a limited income. His first wife, a tailoress, did tailoring work to bring in extra money for the family.[3-5, 9, 14]

The Threat of Air Raids on Plymouth

In the late 1930s, Bill was concerned about the threat of air attack on Plymouth. The increasing speed and range of military aircraft and the city's importance to the Royal Navy made Plymouth a potential target for bombers as the threat of war grew in the late 1930s. The Home

Office had urged local councils to consider how to protect their areas from air attack and in January 1938 the Plymouth City Council debated the proposals for precautions against air attack outlined in the minutes of the Council's Special Purposes Committee.

Bill was fiercely critical of the Council's preparations for air raids, stating 'There has been muddle, drift and incompetency', and moved that the relevant minute be referred back. He declared that there was no protection against bombers and advocated evacuation of the civilian population. 'It will be essential, for instance, to evacuate the public... There may be an opportunity of getting our people out of all this slaughter' Despite his arguments, his amendment was defeated. Convinced of the need to protect Plymouth's population from air raids, Bill joined the Civil Defence Warden's Service in 1938.[15-17]

The Second World War

The Second World War proved that Bill's warnings about the danger of air attack had been prescient. After the fall of France in June 1940, Plymouth was very vulnerable to attack by German aircraft flying from bases in occupied France. The first air raids on Plymouth occurred soon after France's surrender and the attacks increased in intensity. The most devastating air raids on Plymouth took place during March and April 1941. Over nine hundred civilians and many military personnel were killed in these attacks. By April 1941, 1,500 houses had been destroyed while another 15,000 were damaged. The pre-war city centre of Plymouth was nearly obliterated. Only a small number of buildings in the city centre escaped destruction. After the blitzes of spring 1941, many people fled from the city. Its population fell from over 220,000 to 119,000.

By the end of the war 1,172 of Plymouth's civilian population had been killed and over 4,400 wounded. In addition, there were many military casualties. 3,754 houses had been destroyed and over 18,300 badly damaged. The city centre had been reduced to rubble and many of the city's schools, shops, churches and government buildings had been lost. The survey group, Mass Observation, reported in 1941 that the scale of destruction and dislocation in Plymouth was greater than anything they had seen elsewhere in the country.[18]

The Plymouth Blitz

As mentioned earlier, Bill Miller had joined the air raid warden's

Bill Miller watches Jimmy Moses campaigning 1920s

Bill Miller attends the opening of the bathing pool at Tinside on
Plymouth Hoe in October 1935

Plymouth Guildhall Square
From the collection of Plymouth City
Museums & Art Gallery

1947 Labour
Election Leaflet

Bill Miller lays the foundation stone on the first house on the Ham housing estate,
February 1946. Mr Catchpole, the City Architect, is on the right.

Bill Miller
Council election
leaflet 1952

Aneurin Bevan opens a new
Plymouth Housing Estate

Aneurin Bevan opens a new Plymouth Housing Estate.
Bill Miller is leaning forward at the front of the platform

11

Bill Miller helping to award a trophy

Bill Miller speaking at an event

1

service in 1938 and he was head air raid warden in Stonehouse during the heaviest and most intense bombing raids. His own house in East Street, Stonehouse, was hit by a bomb in 1941. He suffered temporary hearing loss as a result of this. His sister-in-law was severely injured and his two younger children had slight injuries. He remained head warden in Stonehouse until August 1941. He displayed great dedication and played an important role in the organisation of the warden service in Stonehouse. He persuaded the army to provide field kitchens in the streets to feed the people and obtained the help of the Marines in clearing the debris left by the air raids. [13-5, 16, 19, 20]

Organising Evacuation - Conflict with the Authorities

Bill's determination to do everything in his power to protect local people from air raids brought him into conflict with the authorities. On his own initiative and without official authority, he organised an unofficial total evacuation. He commandeered buses, lorries and other vehicles and used them to take women and children to safe areas outside the city.

The government had not authorised this evacuation. Bill was arrested for taking the law into his own hands and put on trial. Lady Astor, the famous Conservative M.P. for Plymouth Sutton, was crying and saying 'Bill, they'll send you to prison'. During the trial, he was asked why he had decided to organise the evacuation. He replied that he had told the men in his area who had gone away to fight in the war that he would do his best to protect their wives and families and this was the reason for his actions. The court severely reprimanded him and warned him not to do anything similar in the future. However, only a few days after this court case, the authorities ordered a total evacuation of women and children and Bill felt this vindicated his actions. [3, 4, 20]

Plan for Plymouth

The bombing had devastated Plymouth. Its population had been reduced by almost a half and its city centre had been destroyed. Before the war, there had been severe problems of slum housing and overcrowding in Plymouth and these had been made much worse by the wartime bombing. Once the blitz had ended, it was clear plans had to be made for the postwar reconstruction of the city. In 1941 Plymouth City Council decided to consult an outside expert and asked the advice of Professor Abercrombie, a distinguished academic authority on town planning. Professor Abercrombie and James Paton Watson, the city engineer, worked together on a plan for the postwar reconstruction of Plymouth.

In April 1944 the proposals of Abercrombie and Paton–Watson were presented to Plymouth City Council. The Council created a special committee, called the Reconstruction Committee, in May 1944 to consider the Plan for Plymouth prepared by Abercrombie and Paton-Watson. Bill became one of the members. The Plan for Plymouth was accepted by the Council in September 1944.[21]

Labour's triumph in Plymouth in 1945

In the 1945 General Election, Bill was the election agent of Bert Medland, the Labour Party's candidate in the Plymouth Drake constituency. Labour was triumphant in Plymouth just as it was nationally. Bert Medland won Drake, Sutton elected Lucy Middleton and Michael Foot was victorious in Devonport. Bert Medland paid tribute to Bill's work as his agent.

In the Plymouth City Council elections of November 1945, the Labour Party was also victorious, winning eighteen council seats and becoming the dominant party on the Council for the first time ever. Harry Mason, Bill's old friend, was now Leader of the City Council and Miller became Chairman of the Council's Housing Committee.[22]

Plymouth's Post-war Housing Programme

Bill's Chairmanship of the Housing Committee marked the high point of his career in Plymouth's local politics. For ordinary Plymothians, the most urgent aspect of their city's reconstruction was the construction of new houses to replace the thousands of houses severely damaged during the wartime blitz. Plymouth's housing shortage, already serious before the war, had been made critical by the wartime bombing. In his Plan Professor Abercrombie had proposed building large new housing estates on the city's perimeter.

As Housing Chairman Bill played a key role in Plymouth's massive housebuilding programme in the late 1940s. In the immediate aftermath of the war, it was necessary to build as many houses as possible as quickly as possible and prefabricated houses were built to provide a quick solution to Plymouth's desperate housing shortage. By November 1946, a thousand prefabricated houses had been built in Plymouth.

This was a short-term solution. The longer-term goal was to implement the proposals in the Plan for Plymouth for new housing estates. The building of the first of Plymouth's new post-war housing estates began in November 1945 in Efford (the neighbourhood where the writer has lived since childhood). This was followed by the construction of other new housing estates in Ham, Honicknowle, King's Tamerton, Pennycross, Ernesettle and Whitleigh. These post-war estates were a major improvement on the council housing built in Plymouth before the Second World War.

Bill demonstrated resourcefulness in the way in which he overcame shortages of material and labour which might impede the housing programme. The Admiralty had instructed Royal Dockyards to avoid unemployment by offering to do work for the private sector. Bill and other Councillors met with the Admiral-Superintendent of Devonport Dockyard and other senior Dockyard officials to discuss using Dockyard workers to manufacture items for the city's housing programme. Workers in the Dockyard produced drainpipes, stoves and other items necessary for the new houses.

His dedication to the housing programme was such that, in 1947, he decided not to accept the position of Lord Mayor of Plymouth because it would have meant he would have had to relinquish the Housing Chairmanship. Thousands of Plymothians desperately needed housing and he felt he could best serve the people of the city by remaining as Chairman. He worked tirelessly, travelling frequently to Whitehall and seeing many housing applicants in his own home.

Between the end of the war in 1945 and March 1950, 6,832 permanent and temporary houses were built or rebuilt in Plymouth. Plymouth ranked fifth among county boroughs in terms of the total number of houses built and third when the scale of housebuilding was related to the size of the population. The Council had been responsible for the great bulk of the house-building. Plymouth local authority had completed 3,470 permanent new dwellings while over a thousand more were under construction. It had also built 2,250 temporary houses. Bill contributed more than anyone else to the success of the housing programme.[5, 6, 20, 23]

Bill's Vision of Housing for Plymouth
Bill Miller was a visionary. He saw the aim of the housing programme he presided over as not only the construction of new houses but the

creation of new communities. In a speech which he gave in Efford in October 1946, he declared 'We do not only want to build houses but to create homes in which our future citizens will be moulded'.

The proposals contained in the Plan for Plymouth were heavily influenced by the ideas of neighbourhood unit planning. Professor Abercrombie was a keen advocate of the neighbourhood unit concept. The idea was that urban areas should be divided up into urban villages. Each would have several thousand inhabitants and be based around social institutions and facilities such as a village green, shops, schools and churches in order to ensure that they became genuine communities. It was intended that Efford and the other housing estates would develop into neighbourhoods of this type.

Bill strongly supported the neighbourhood unit concept and Plymouth's postwar housing estates were based on these principles. He told Laurence Thompson '. . . you must understand we built all our houses on the neighbourhood principle . . . Everything complete in the neighbourhood, you see, nothing more than ten minutes' walk from the farthest house on the estate.' It was a vision of community which Bill tried to translate into reality. [24]

Miller's growing reputation
Bill Miller's achievements were recognised not only in Plymouth but at national level. In the 1946 New Year's Honours List, he was awarded a BEM. He received the OBE in 1947 and he was given the CBE in the New Year's Honours List of 1948. He became a member of the National Housing Council and the Housing Committee of the Association of Municipal Corporations.

He had close personal relationships with the leading figures of the postwar Labour government. On one occasion he was seen deep in conversation with the Prime Minister, Clement Attlee. He became a close personal friend of Aneurin Bevan, the Minister for Health and Housing. He came to know Harold Wilson when Wilson was Minister of Works and the two men worked closely together to provide the technicians and skilled building workers needed for the housing programme in Plymouth. [3, 17, 25]

Council Activities in the 1950s
The Tories won a majority on the Plymouth Council in 1949 and increased their majority in the local elections of 1950. In 1950, Bill

was narrowly defeated by his Tory opponent and lost his seat in Charles ward. The local paper, *Western Evening Herald*, observed that many would regret his defeat because of his 'yeoman service' to Plymouth. [26]

However, Miller soon returned to the Council. In May 1951, he won a by-election in Sutton ward. When Labour regained control of Plymouth Council in 1953, He again became Chair of the Housing Committee and occupied this position until 1959. New housing developments were begun in Manadon Vale and in the historic area of the Barbican and preparations were made for the very large housing estate in Southway which was built in the 1960s. He also served on the Reconstruction and the Street Lighting Committees in the 1950s.

In 1959, he was elected Chairman of the National Housing and Town Planning Council and attended two world congresses of that organisation.

The 1960s
In 1962, he served as Deputy Lord Mayor to Harry Mason, his childhood friend, who was Lord Mayor for the second time. In 1963, Eric Nuttall succeeded Miller as Chair of Housing and Bill became Chair of the Parks and Recreations Committee.

He remained a City Councillor until only a few months before his death. He finally retired from Plymouth Council in May 1970. He died on 21 December 1970 at the age of eighty. [5, 6, 27]

Bill Miller's Political Contribution
Bill Miller's career in the local politics of Plymouth was a remarkable one. He combined vision and imagination with impressive organisational skills and a great capacity for hard work. His talents were displayed to the full when he presided over Plymouth's postwar house-building programme. He was Housing Chair at a time when the City desperately needed houses, but Bill saw his task as being more than building houses as quickly as possible and was inspired by a desire to create communities. As he said to Laurence Thompson, "Don't you see we're not just building houses, we're making homes". Bill Miller's work had a seminal influence on Plymouth's postwar development and he should be seen as an important figure in the City's Twentieth Century history. [28]

FOOTNOTES

(1) Laurence Thompson, 'Portrait of England: News From Somewhere' Victor Gollancz, London. 1952. pp 19-20

(2) Thompson, op.cit. p.13

(3) Interview with Councillor Claude Miller 1995

(4) Interview with Councillor Claude Miller June 30 2002

(5) 'Leader of post-war homes drive dies'. Western Morning News. Tuesday, December 22 1970. page 3.

(6) 'Mr W.A. Miller, leader of city homes drive, dies'. Western Evening Herald. Tuesday, December 22 1970. p. 3

(7) Mark Brayshay,'Plymouth's Past: So Worthy and Peerless a Western Port 'in Brian Chalkley, David Dunkerley and Peter Gripaios (editors). 'Plymouth: Maritime City in Transition'. David and Charles. 1991. p.60

(8) Crispin Gill, 'Plymouth. A New History. 1603 to the present day.' Vol 2. David and Charles. 1979. p.174

(9) Gill op.cit. p.181

(10) Gill op.cit. p176-177

(11) 'Drake's First Labour Member,' Western Evening Herald. May 31 1929.

(12) Chris Bryant. 'Stafford Cripps.The First Modern Chancellor'. Hodder and Stoughton. London 1997. p. 80; Simon Burgess. 'Stafford Cripps. A political life'. Victor Gollancz. 1999. pp. 45-46; Eric Estorick. 'Stafford Cripps. A Biography'. William Heinemann. 1949. pp 79-80

(13) The trial of the election petition for the Drake Division of the Borough of Plymouth. Minutes of the proceedings before Justices Swift and Talbot, the Guildhall, Plymouth, Thursday 17 October 1929, Tuesday 22 October 1929, Friday 25 October 1929; 'Drake Petition'. Western Evening Herald. October 22 1929, p.8; 'Mr Moses' Election Agent in the Witness-Box'. Western Evening Herald. October 23 1929, p.1; 'Judgement Against the Petitioners'. Western Evening Herald. October 25 1929.

(14) 'Twelve Thousand Margin in Drake'. Western Evening Herald. October 28 1931. p.1 Colin Rallings and Michael Thrasher. 'Plymouth's Politics'. In Chalkley, Dunkerley and Gripaios. op.cit. p.158

(15) 'Air Raid Precautions for Plymouth'. Western Evening Herald. January 11 1938. p.4

(16) 'Many West Awards in Honours List'. Western Evening Herald. January 9 1946

(17) Alderman Miller may be next Lord Mayor'. Western Evening Herald. September 4 1947

(18) Brian Chalkley and John Goodridge. The 1943 Plan for Plymouth.

War-Time Vision and Post –War Realities. In Chalkley, Dunkerley and Gripaios. op.cit. pp 62-64; Gill. op.cit. pp 194-197

(19) Thompson. op.cit. p.20

(20) 'A wise eye on the city' by Martin Freeman. Martin Freeman's interview with Councillor Claude Miller in the Evening Herald, June 20 2003. p.6

(21) Gill. op. cit. pp197- 198; Chalkley and Goodridge. op. cit. pp. 66-71

(22) Gill. op.cit. pp 199, 215-216; Rallings and Thrasher. op.cit. pp. 158-159. 'Labour scores Triple Gain at Plymouth'. Western Evening Herald. July 26 1945. p.1 'Big victory over Wealth and Rank'. Western Evening Herald. July 26th 1945. p.3 'Labour Obtains First-Time Lead in Plymouth's Council'. Western Evening Herald, November 2 1945. p.2; 'Plymouth to have three by-elections.' Western Evening Herald. November 1945. p.3

(23) Thompson. op.cit. pp 13-14, 20-21; Gill. op.cit. p.199; Chalkley and Goodridge. op.cit. pp 76-79; 'Devonport Dockyard Housing 'Switch' to avoid discharges'; 'Alderman Miller's 'No' to Lord Mayoralty'. Western Evening Herald. September 5 1947; 'Plymouth has provided 6,832 houses.' Western Evening Herald. May 8 1950. p.3

(24) 'Efford's Permanent Homes'. Western Evening Herald. October 2 1946; Chalkley and Goodridge. op.cit. pp 77-79; Thompson. op.cit. pp. 14-15

(25) 'Westcountry Folk in New Year's Honours List. Plymouth's Housing Chairman'. Western Evening Herald. Thursday January 1 1948

(26) 'Tories gain 4 Seats, raise City Council majority to ten. Mr. W. A. Miller is among Labour casualties at Plymouth'. Western Evening Herald. 12 May 1950; 'A Citizen's Diary'. Western Evening Herald. 13 May 1950

(27) 'Sutton Re-elect a Labour Councillor. Mr W.A. Miller has Majority of 943 over Conservative.' Western Evening Herald. May 4 1951. p.2

(28) Thompson. op.cit. p.19

COUNCILLOR CLAUDE MILLER

Claude Miller was born in Plymouth on 23 March 1915. His active involvement in Labour Party politics began when he was 16 and helped to establish a branch of the Labour League of Youth in Plymouth. During the Second World War Claude joined the RAF and was assigned to electrical work on aircraft. In 1941 he married Norah Caroline Symons and their marriage lasted until her death in 1987.

After the War in 1946 Claude and his brother-in-law opened a radio and electrical goods retail business. Claude was also active in the community. He became a Justice of the Peace in 1968 and served in this capacity until 1985. In the early 1970s he became chair of the management group which ran the Youth and Community Centre in the Efford area of Plymouth.

In the Devon County Council elections of 1981 Claude was elected as a Labour and Co-operative Councillor in Efford ward. He was a very active County Councillor. He became Labour's spokesperson on libraries and served as the County Council representative for Plymouth on the Plymouth Health Authority. In particular, Claude played a leading role in social services, and was exceptionally thorough in his inspection of care homes. He earned a reputation as the champion of the elderly. When Devon County Council proposed